READ WITH
Biff,
Chip &
Kipper

Levels 1-2
Reading Skills Activity Book

This book belongs to ...

....

Written by Kate Ruttle, based on the
original characters created by
Roderick Hunt and Alex Brychta

OXFORD
UNIVERSITY PRESS

Who's who?

Read the names of the family in the picture below.
Write their names in the spaces next to the right picture.

Mum **Dad** **Biff** **Chip** **Kipper** **Floppy**

Why? Learning to recognise that a character or image is essentially the same, even when it appears in different positions, is an important skill for early reading.

Which Floppy is which?

Join Floppy to his matching shadow or outline. Look carefully to make sure it's the right one.
Then colour in the outlines.

What is Kipper's favourite toy?

Join the alphabet dots in the right order
to find Kipper's favourite toy. Colour in the toy.

a b c d e f g h i j k l m n
o p q r s t u v w x y z

Why? Children need to know alphabetical order, letter names and letter sounds. This activity helps children practise these skills, as well as pencil control.

Tell a story

Number these pictures 1, 2, 3, so they tell a story. What is happening in each picture?

Draw what you think will happen after Floppy smells the cake.

Why? Asking children to think about the order of events is one way of helping them to understand the story.

Who's got what?

Wilma made a snowman and her friends are bringing things to dress it up. What do you think they've all got?

Tip: Find the stickers to show what everyone is carrying.

Can you make these pictures the same?

What can you see in and around Kipper's paddling pool? Use the stickers to make the pictures the same.

Why? Looking for small visual differences helps children learn to look for similarities and differences between different words.

8

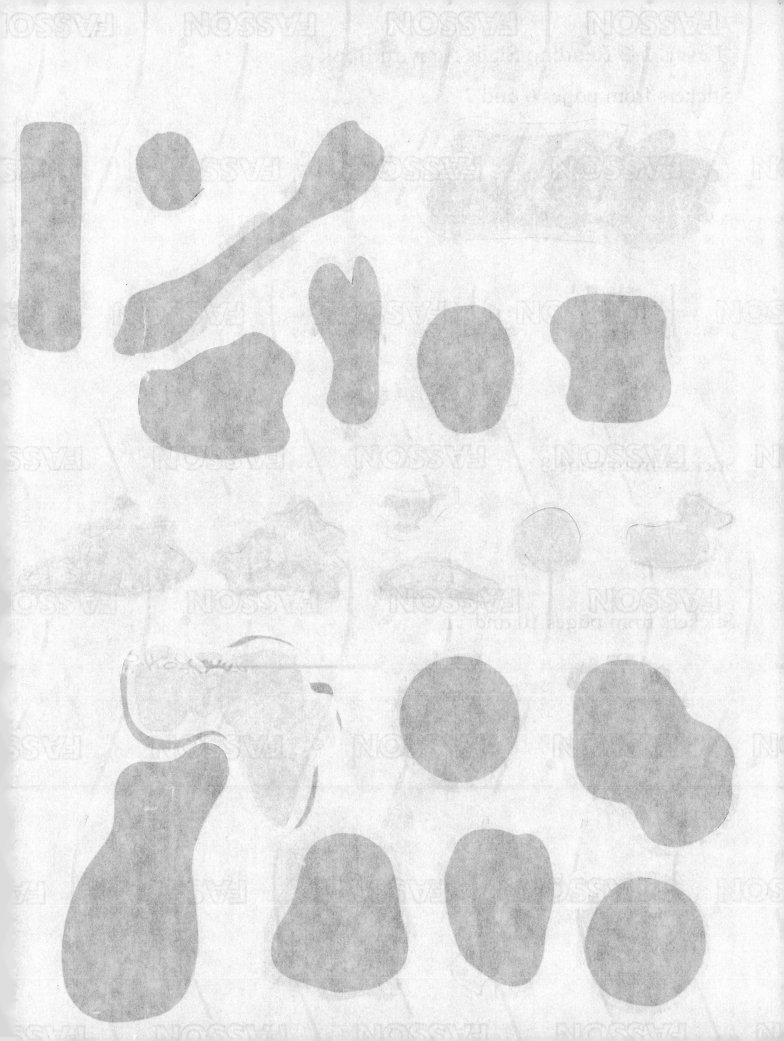

Levels 1-2 Reading Skills Activity Book

Stickers from pages 6 and 7

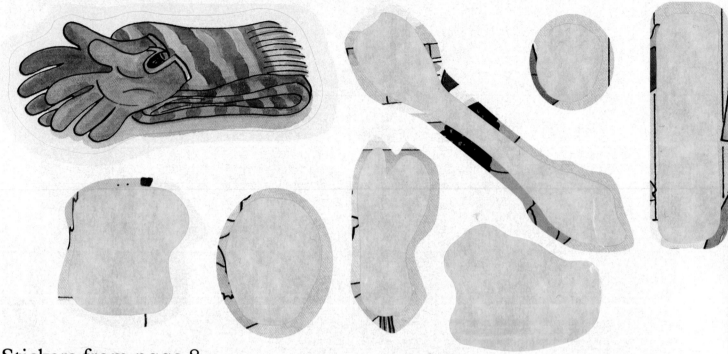

Stickers from page 8

Stickers from pages 10 and 11

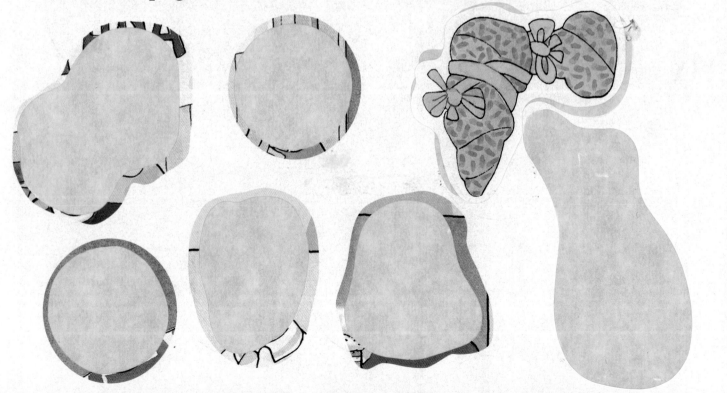

Snowmen twins

Put a tick beside the two snowmen which are exactly the same.

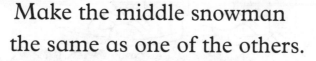

Make the middle snowman the same as one of the others.

Why? Looking for small visual differences helps children learn to look for similarities and differences between different words.

9

Who came to Dad's party?

It's Dad's birthday and he's having a party.
Who do you think will be there?

Tip: Talk about who came to Dad's party. Put the faces on the right people. Can you also find two present stickers?

Spot the difference

There are 6 differences between the two pictures.
Circle the differences in the top picture.

Why? This links to the activities on pages 8 and 9, developing an eye for detail, which helps children look for similarities and differences between words.

A maze

Follow the maze to help Floppy find his bone.

Why? This activity helps children to look ahead, which is a vital skill for reading. You can also encourage them to trace the maze to develop pencil control.

Word search

Read the names in the boxes under the picture.
Find and circle all the names in the word search.

Biff   **Chip**   **Wilma**   **Wilf**   **Kipper**   **Floppy**

F	l	o	p	p	y	l
a	n	d	s	M	u	m
i	t	B	i	f	f	k
K	i	p	p	e	r	A
b	s	d	C	h	i	p
o	n	D	a	d	i	s
i	n	W	i	l	m	a
a	W	i	l	f	n	o

Can you find any
other names?

Why? In this activity children have to look carefully at both letter
shapes and sequences of letters. The words are arranged from left
to right to support reading and writing.

14

Make them the same

Draw a line to match each outline to the right coloured parcel. Then colour in the outlines to make them the same as the coloured parcels.

Talk about what might be inside each parcel.

Why? This activity develops an awareness of shape and pattern.

15

counting

Look at the picture and the objects below. Count how many of each thing you can see. Write the number in the boxes.

How many ...

grasshoppers? ☑

sheep? ☑

children? ☐

cups? ☑

sandwiches? ☑

1 2 3 4 5 6 7 8 9 10

Why? Looking carefully at pictures and finding details is good practice for recognising letter patterns and shapes in words.